Unreported Truth:
Climate Hoax 2030

Global Warming, Fear Politics and a Totalitarian
Techno-Fascist Future?

Agenda 21 – The Great Reset – The Green deal
Exposed!

Rebel Press Media

Disclaimer

Our other books

Check out our other books for other unreported news, exposed facts and debunked truths, and more.

Join the exclusive Rebel Press Media Circle!

You will get new updates about the unreported reality delivered in your inbox every Friday.

Sign up here today:

https://campsite.bio/rebelpressmedia

Introduction

After using "only" 100 nuclear bombs, 15 to 35 million tons of soot will be released into the atmosphere, according to the IPPNW, causing at least 2 billion people to starve to death. - The globalist climate sect can't be that evil, right?

Nobody benefits from a nuclear war, so it will never break out. At least, that is the thinking of the vast majority of people, and one of the reasons why the tensions around Ukraine are not really taken seriously. However, there are other voices warning that the globalist climate-vaccine sect that has gained almost total control over the West in a short period of time is actually pushing for a nuclear war, because it would decimate humanity in one fell swoop. Conspiracy theory? Perhaps, but on March 3, 2011, we pointed in an article to NASA scientists who suggested that a 'limited' nuclear war with no more than 50 to 100 nuclear bombs would stop Global Warming and reverse it into Global Cooling (which, incidentally, has already begun even without a nuclear war).

The well-known international monthly magazine National Geographic wrote about 10 years ago that, according to NASA scientists, the world will cool by 1.25 degrees in the 2-3 years following a small nuclear war. In tropical areas, the temperature drop could even reach 4 degrees.

That's because some 15 to 35 million tons of soot and smoke will be released into the atmosphere as a result of 100 small nuclear explosions*, which will obscure sunlight. The mild nuclear winter that then ensues will have devastating effects on crops, and cause mass starvation. Precipitation (rain) will be reduced by 10%, and the ozone layer will be severely damaged, allowing harmful ultraviolet radiation to penetrate to the Earth's surface.

(* Similar to the bomb that destroyed Hiroshima. That one had a power of only 15 kilotons. One warhead from a Russian RS-24 missile is 150 to 500 kilotons strong.)

Rationing and travel restrictions

If nuclear war is perhaps not such a good idea after all, the quiver of the international climate sect contains a few other delusions to counter the fictitious specter of CO2-induced Global Warming. For example, how about the proposal made by "experts" at the international climate conference in Cancun in 2010 to introduce strict food and energy rations and travel restrictions for all residents in developed countries.

Travel restrictions were unthinkable until the early 2020s, until... (enfin, you know). Of course, all these restrictions only affect ordinary citizens and SMEs, and never the ruling elite who supposedly have "the best interests of the world" at heart. They always exclude themselves from such extremely radical and painful measures.

Chemtrails

In Cancun it was seriously considered to switch to 'plan B' if international treaties on reducing CO2 failed, and to (continue to) spray - according to critics - substances such as aluminum and barium into the atmosphere ('chemtrails'), with which one hopes to block sunlight. (2) The existence of 'chemtrails' has been amply proven, but is still dismissed as a 'conspiracy theory' in the mainstream media.

A recent test planned in Sweden by Bill 'vaccine' Gates to dim the sun by releasing calcium carbonate particles into the atmosphere was cancelled after much protest. 'You can't test the detonator of a bomb and then say this can't possibly hurt,' responded Niclas Hällström, director of the 'green' Swedish think tank WhatNext?

Global Cooling

Contrary to what the establishment claims, climate change has always been a permanent process that never stops. The mild warming of the last century was very welcome after the 'Dalton Minimum', and moreover in no way deviating from normal fluctuations. Unfortunately, all signs point to a new solar minimum pushing us into a potentially very prolonged period of Global Cooling, which by definition is bad news for humanity (cold = worse crops, more diseases, more deaths and more wars).

Therefore, international CO2 climate policy is only a means to eventually force all of humanity into an all-encompassing and all-controlling fascist one-world system. This is why the world's population is still being led to believe that "something urgently needs to be done" about climate change, while the solar cycle in combination with our planet's diminishing magnetic field is the real, impossible to influence cause.

Nuclear war serious option for climate elite?

Bill Gates has never made a secret of his belief that there are far too many people on Earth, and that action (such as mass mandatory vaccinations) should be taken to significantly reduce that number. It is therefore no longer inconceivable that these kinds of lunatics, who have gained so much power over countries and organizations, would even consider a "limited" nuclear war as a serious option to get rid of a large part of humanity in one fell swoop. After a few years, they will then emerge from their ultra-luxurious bunker complexes, to realize their own dream world on the rubble.

In 2013, the Nobel Prize-winning organization International Physicians for the Prevention of Nuclear War warned that even the limited use of nuclear war will end human civilization. The use of 100 nuclear bombs will create a global famine that will kill 2 billion people. New calculations from 2019 paint an even bleaker picture: not 5 million, but 15 to 35 million tons of soot will be released into the atmosphere, making the consequences even more disastrous.

Fortunately, history - especially that since the beginning of last century - has shown us that people with intensely evil ideas never have the chance to get into the lead and actually carry out their drive for destruction... right?

Table of Contents

Chapter 1: Global cooling?

Bitter weather and unprecedented volumes of snow fell in Northern Europe, Russia, China, South Asia, Japan, Alaska, the United States, and Australia this winter.

In December 2020, the average worldwide temperature plummeted by 0.26 degrees Celsius in one month, reaching barely 0.27 degrees above the baseline. While Global Cooling has begun and multiple cold and snow records are being broken throughout the world, Bill Gates is supporting a proposal to actually limit sunlight—all while the top section of the Northern Hemisphere, including Europe, will be longing for warmth in a few years. Heat, which will be in short supply in the West due to the prohibition of gas, oil, and nuclear energy. (China, on the other hand, is hoarding natural gas in large quantities.)

The sun has returned to ice-cold silence after a short rebirth at the end of last year, and there are no visible sunspots today. The last solar cycle (No.24), the longest and weakest in nearly a century, served as a strong warning. NASA anticipates that cycle 25 will be even weaker. All historical tendencies indicate that the current phase of Global Cooling, known colloquially as the 'Eddy Minimum,' will result in a new Little Ice Age.

In any event, the next several decades will be increasingly frigid. We have observed the impact of a weaker sun and a dwindling magnetic field surrounding the Earth in increasingly irregular weather in recent years. Extreme heat and drought, or extreme cold and/or a lot of snow, vary widely by location and are part of Global Cooling.

A selection of objectively verifiable recent weather this winter and climate news highlights what is truly happening on our planet:

* **British snowstorm** - Only three weeks after the British Meteorological Office announced that there will be almost no more snow and freezing temperatures by 2040-2060, hundreds of motorists had to be rescued from their automobiles in the Derbyshire Peak District and Cheshire due to a surprise snowstorm. Snow, according to previous estimates for 2000, 2012, and 2020, would be a thing of the past, and the Arctic would be ice-free. The exact opposite has occurred. On December 28, this is what 'global warming' looked like on the British edition of KNMI:

* **Extreme cold is forecast in the United Kingdom.** The blizzard appears to be a foreshadowing of the worst winter in at least ten years, with temperatures dropping below -20 C. It is not out of the question that the cold records of 1941 and 1962 will be broken. 'Ice pancakes' developed in Scotland, a rare phenomena that only occurs in very cold seas, such as those off Canada and the Baltic Sea (The Baltic).

*** -43.3 degrees Celsius in Norway and -41.1 degrees Celsius in Finland.** On December 28, the temperature in northern Norway plummeted to -43.3 degrees Celsius. It hasn't gotten this cold there since 2001. In neighboring Finland, the temperature in the north dropped to -41.1 degrees Celsius, the coldest since 1995.

*** At least 20 weather stations in China set new low temperatures in December.** The temperature at Beijing's Foyeding station was -26.4 degrees Celsius, a new record, and the temperature in Shanghai Pudon was -6.2 degrees Celsius. Temperatures in certain regions of the country fell by 18 degrees Celsius in one day on Wednesday. In the Northeast and South, the average temperature will be at least 5 degrees lower than normal. Because of the strong demand for electricity (heat), Beijing has reopened an outdated coal-fired power plant. The Government has also declared that it will maximize gas output and import record volumes of LNG (liquefied natural gas).

*** Horokanai, Japan, has set a new monthly cold record of -32.6 degrees Celsius.** Recently, snowfall of up to 4 meters is anticipated in portions of northern and eastern Japan. In mid-December, 1 to 2 meters of snow had already fallen in several areas, and records had been broken in a number of places, including the southwest.

* **Alaska's most powerful winter cyclone ever:** On Twitter, climatologist Brian Brettschneider claimed that the giant storm in Alaska has plummeted the barometer to 921 mb, a new low record. The previous high-water mark (925 mb) was set in 1977. The west coast of Canada and the northwestern United States should brace themselves for meters of snowfall in the coming days and weeks; Canada's Baffin Island was already hammered by a very strong blizzard last Sunday, which ECCC meteorologists described as "quite rare" for December;

* **Keep track of high pressure while it's really cold outside**. Mongolia. Mongolia set a new preliminary high pressure world record of 1094.3 millibars. This occurred during a period of severely cold weather (-45.5 C.). Temperatures of -45 to -50, and even lower, have been recorded in wide portions of Asia during the last week.

* **Extremely chilly in subtropical Mexico:** dwellers on the peninsula cum tourist paradise of Yucatán had to haul out seldom used blankets. In reality, it barely reached 8 degrees in Motul. The former record of 5 degrees from 1971, according to meteorologist Juan Vázquez Montalvo, might be beaten this month.

* **Cargo ship stranded in heavy sea ice:** On December 13, the 9490-ton Russian cargo ship Sparta-III was detained for days in Yenisey Bay in nearly 1 meter thick sea ice. To free the ship, a nuclear icebreaker was needed.

Last month, 80 percent of Russia endured record freezing temperatures of up to -50 degrees Celsius. That, however, will not be found in the mainstream media. The 38 degrees measured in Verkhoyansk were extensively misreported in June 2020. However, extreme temperatures are not unusual; summer temperatures of 30 degrees or more are common; in 1915, the temperature hit 37.8 degrees.

The global temperature has plummeted to barely 0.2 degrees above normal.

This blast of bitter cold and heavy snowfall has spread to Kazakhstan, Japan, Alaska, Canada, and even Florida. Snowfall totals set new records in Iceland, the Alps, Canada, and southern Asia. Almost the whole southern hemisphere of Australia turned extremely chilly.

For the past 30, 40 years, entire generations have been terrified by the so-called melting of the ice caps caused by the now-completely disproved CO2-Global Warming hoax. However, according to the Climate Change Institute at the University of Maine, global temperatures are still only 0.2 degrees above the 1979-2000 average, which is not even close to the catastrophic warming that has been predicted for 30 years but has not arrived and, as all evidence now indicates, will never arrive.

The necessary era of warming is coming to an end, but the West is not prepared.

On the contrary, the comparably brief era of much-needed mild warming since the Dalton Minimum, which allowed our civilization to develop, has come to an end. We may have the technological means to properly arm ourselves against cold and all its consequences at this time, but those means - known as 'fossil' energy - will be dismantled in the next 10 to 30 years, and replaced by extremely weather-dependent and prohibitively expensive windmills, solar panels, and heat pumps (which do not work in the event of a major frost). Simultaneously, our trees will be fueled by biomass power plants.

The planet will need heat, but Gates wants to limit the sun's rays.

To make matters worse, multimillionaire Bill "vaccine" Gates, who has no background in climate science (or any other science for that matter), wants to dim the sun's rays, making it more colder, with much more disastrous consequences for humanity (disease outbreaks and pandemics, crop failures and famines, collapse of world trade, mass mortality of the elderly and weak, wars over scarce food supplies).

Gates is supporting a Harvard University research called "SCoPEx" (Stratospheric Controlled Perturbation Experiment) that would use calcium carbonate dust particles to block sunlight. A test balloon will be flown in Sweden in 2021 or 2022, dispersing 2 kilograms of this 'non-toxic' chemical into the atmosphere. Whether you believe in the climate/global warming religion or not, tampering with the immensely complex climate is a poor idea, since the repercussions might be unforeseeable and devastating.

'You can't test a bomb's detonator and then claim it can't possibly injure,' said Niclas Hällström, director of Sweden's 'green' think tank.

But, at a time when the well-known Orwellian creeds 'War is Peace,' 'Freedom is Slavery,' and 'Ignorance is Strength' have been expanded to include 'Cooling is Warming,' we should not be surprised that governments are unwilling to consider that their climate policies based on zero CO2 emissions and stopping 'warming' are not only a complete waste of money, but also a complete waste of time.

Chapter 2: State of forced emergency?

Facts and observations, such as the "historically" named snowfall of sometimes more than 4 meters thick in the Alpine region last week, no longer count. Ideology has completely supplanted real science, common sense and even observation with our own eyes - Current climate policies will cause West to collapse 'and not rise for 600 years' - Everyone must give up wealth and freedom for zero CO2, while super-rich get even richer.

Anyone who takes a moment to pull their head out of the swamp of the mainstream media and does 15 minutes of background research on independent and free news sources knows that the emergency bill and the strict measures associated with it have nothing at all to do with public health, but are part of enforced behavioral change under UN Agenda 21/2030. This seems to have succeeded to such an extent - after all, 9 out of 10 people still blindly follow all corona orders, no matter how senseless and diametric they are - that UN Secretary-General António Guterres dared to reveal the real reason for the corona pandemic hoax: he wants to declare a permanent climate emergency until 2050.

Guterres repeated the nonsense propaganda debunked by numerous scientists that "if we do nothing, we are heading for a catastrophic temperature increase of more than 3 degrees this century. The margin of error of the IPCC climate models on which this is based is immense. No one can claim with any degree of certainty how the climate will develop on the basis of these computer models. So far, therefore, hardly anything of these models turns out to be correct.

The North Pole should have been ice free by 2014

Al Gore, another 'climate leader', predicted 11 years ago that the North Pole would be completely ice-free in 2014 according to his computer model. All attendees at the COP15 Climate Conference in Copenhagen seemed to swallow this scaremongering like sweet bread, and promised to take measures to reduce CO2 emissions. Gore said that "only reckless idiots" would ignore the melting of the polar ice.

But at the end of 2020, who turned out to be the real idiot (yet again)? This summer, the polar ice barely dropped below 5,000 km2, and even began to increase at record rates from September onwards. But instead of apologizing, the international CAGW (anthropogenic warming) camp cheerfully continues to spread fear and lies. For example, in 2018, Greenpeace repeated yet again that we only have "12 years left to save the world. (2)

Ideology has supplanted science and perception

The UN specifically set up the quasi-scientific IPCC to push the CO2 agenda through. This has been a purely political decision that in fact created the beginning of a kind of communist world government, which in the next

10 years must actually gain power in all countries, starting with the West.

Facts are no longer relevant in this regard. Ideology has supplanted not only science and common sense, but even observation with our own eyes. The countless cold and snow records that have been broken recently - parts of France, Italy, Austria and Switzerland were covered this week with 'historic' snow totaling more than 4 meters, and rare summer snow fell in New Zealand last Friday,- are ignored, or attributed with dry eyes to 'warming'.

What is the sun doing?

The real reason is a many thousands of years old and fully proven climate cycle, and a now starting (relative) solar minimum, with the according to NASA 'weakest solar cycle in the last 200 years'. This all points to substantial cooling, not warming. It is even conceivable that we are at the beginning of a new Ice Age.

However, because of some recently appeared sunspots and sudden eruptions, some scientists think that the current solar cycle may yet become (temporarily) more active, which because of the Earth's diminished protective magnetic field would be bad news for humanity, especially since we have become so dependent on electronics. One big solar eruption our way, and half the planet could be permanently shrouded in darkness by ruined electrical systems.

UN wants climate emergency until 2050

But the UN Secretary-General continues to live in his own fantasy world, and now even demands that "every country, every city, every financial institution and every business must adopt plans so that (CO2) emissions are at zero net by 2050. This, he says, must be started immediately by declaring a "climate emergency" in all countries, until "climate neutrality is achieved.

That means new lockdowns over the next few years, until after the next lockdown there is no economy and no work left to return to.

The EU, of course, is once again at the forefront of breaking down our stable energy supply and thus our economy and society, and promised to reduce CO2 emissions by at least 55% by 2030 compared to the year 1990.

West will not rise after collapse due to climate policy 'for 600 years'

'These people (Klaus Schwab, Bill Gates, Antonio Guterres, Frans Timmermans, etc.) are extremely dangerous,' warns American economist Martin Armstrong. 'They have no idea what they are doing. As for the West, it will never get up (after the collapse due to climate policy) for 600 years. They are using the lockdowns not for a virus, but for climate change.'

The decline of Western civilization, by the way, is proceeding exactly according to 'The Fourth Turning' (1997), in which William Strauss and Neil Howe showed, using 500 years of Western history, that the rise and fall of a civilization follows certain processes and patterns, which cannot be avoided time and time again. According to them, these historical laws will lead to the collapse of Western civilization in (or around) 2025.

Armstrong: 'They think they can simply rebuild the economy in a short time ('big back better') and hand out money to those who have lost their jobs. They never figured out that they would totally destroy our way of life with these lockdowns, and that even by the greatest imagination there will NEVER be a return to 'normal'.'

Everyone has to give up wealth for zero CO2, while super-rich get even richer

'Big Tech is behind them, because they will replace the banks and eliminate all competition (SMEs)... Soon all your food will be delivered to your home, and you will never drive to a store again unless you have an electric car. But again: they don't have enough power to do that.' Yet several Western are already banning internal combustion engines from 2030.

'The arrogance of these people who, as soon as they became super-rich, would help bring about 'equality' by ending capitalism, while retaining their own wealth, is

20

mind-boggling. These people, who think they can
remake society, will never have a hard time in their
lives. They are responsible for all the suicides because
people have lost everything. In Japan, there are more
deaths by suicide than by Covid. They never figured out
that at least 40% can't work at home, nor what would
happen to them. It was just about achieving ZERO CO2.'

'Tyranny is the cruel, unreasonable or arbitrary use of
power or control in the hand of someone or a group of
tyrants, who consider themselves better than everyone
else. These tyrants should look at history. Then they will
see that they will be driven out of their haughty seats,
and will be lucky if their heads stay on them then.'

Chapter 3: A new ice age?

Our temperature is regulated by the sun - Is the very uncommon conjunction of Jupiter and Saturn on December 21 (the last time it happened around 800 years ago) a forerunner of a new Ice Age?

The corona 'pandemic' scam is essentially a component of what may be the greatest scam humankind has ever faced: global warming (due to anthropogenic CO_2). In reality, over thousands of years, the climate has cycled from cold to warm and back again. Every 179 years or so, the environment cools dramatically and becomes much wetter. A Little Ice Age occurs every 360 years. Such an Ice Age occurs every 1440 years (4 x 360 years), while a major Great Ice Age occurs every 11,520 years (8 × 1440 years). And guess what? All of these cycles, including the possibility of a new Great Ice Age, are converging right now. And no amount of climate policy, no matter how expensive, will be able to change that. We can prepare, but our government is doing the opposite, weakening our technical protections against extreme cold.

The 179-year cycle was proven in landmark investigations by geologists and astronomers W. Fairbridge and John E. Sanders of Columbia University. This cycle is generated by the sun's retrograde (clockwise) motion around the solar system's barycenter (center of gravity), which causes variations in both the speed of rotation and the sun's emission, which reduces dramatically after each cycle.

'The undeniable solar cycle is a reality of existence.'

The gravitational force of the planets, particularly the two biggest, Jupiter and Saturn, causes the sun's retrograde motion. When the two planets are in the same quadrant of the solar system, they exert a combined gravitational force on the sun that is significantly stronger. 'This cycle is undeniable,' asserted the two academics (em.). 'The solar cycle must now be accepted as a given.'

It will be there after sunset on December 21, the first day of winter. Jupiter and Saturn will appear as a double planet in the sky for the first time since 1226. Although the planets come near together roughly once every 20 years as seen from Earth, the conjunction on December 21 is extremely unusual.

Dr. Theodor Landscheidt, the founder of the Schroeter Institut für Erforschung der Zyklen der Sonnenaktivität in Waldmünchen, Germany, was widely regarded as the world's foremost authority on solar retrogradation. Other scientists and astronomers discovered that his projections for the time beginning in 1979 were 90% accurate. For example, in 1984, he predicted that solar activity would fall in 1990, which occurred.

23

The solar retrograde alters the star's geomagnetic field, causing sudden climatic shifts on Earth. These changes are so dramatic that our planet repeatedly enters a Little Ice Age once every 360 years.

Little Ice Ages are always accompanied by the collapse of civilizations.

According to geological study, the 360-year Little Ice Age cycle may be traced all the way back to the Jurassic era (200 to 145 million years ago). 'It corresponds with the fall of the Roman Empire,' study geologist Jack Sauers remarked. 'It corresponds to the end of the Sumerian Empire.' It corresponds to the demise of the Ottoman Empire (when Genghis Khan invaded from the north). It corresponds to the demise of the Greek Empire. And it now corresponds with the demise of multiple major civilizations.'

Regrettably for us, the previous Little Ice Age occurred almost precisely 360 years ago. 'If this pattern persists, a comparable Little Ice Age... can be predicted early in the twenty-first century,' Fairbridge and Sanders said. And that's precisely what we've been seeing in recent years: unpredictable weather patterns are the first indicators of a new long-term trend of declining temperatures, caused by the oncoming solar minimum.

Also marks the start of a new Great Ice Age cycle.

However, it does not end there. After three Little Ice Ages, or every 1440 years, another severe Little Ice Age will occur, with "dramatic and quick" climate changes such as high dryness and/or heat in one place and excessive wetness and/or cold in another. This cycle was identified while studying the Greenland ice sheet. Paul Mayewski reported his findings in the Journal of Geophysical Research in 1997. Deep-sea drill samples from the North Atlantic have likewise revealed the 1440-year span.

Our climate became extremely frigid around 4200 years ago, as it had done 2800 and 1400 years before. That suggests we're about to enter another incredibly chilly Little Ice Age. If that isn't enough, there is also the broader climate/ice age cycle of 11,520 years (8 phases of 1440 years) and the Great Ice Age cycle of 100,000 years. And, you got it, it has now been around 11,500 and 100,000 years since they last occurred. (1)

As a result, it is absurd that the world is now concerned about Global Warming, says Robert Felix in "Not by Fire, but by Ice." Instead, we must begin planning for really cold periods, which have historically caused considerably more difficulties than periods when the climate is warming. Warming always leads to the flourishing of civilizations; cooling, on the other hand, invariably leads to the reverse. Even if the temperature lowers by a few degrees, most crops will fail, resulting in widespread starvation and death. Scarcity of food also causes big conflicts and wars.

Cold-protection technology is being systematically removed.

Fortunately, we can prepare ourselves technologically for this terrible cold by using oil, gas, and nuclear energy. But, before you exhale a sigh of relief, these stable, weather-independent energy sources will be phased out in the next 10, 20 years and replaced with solar panels and wind turbines, which will soon freeze to bits and/or be buried by a heavy coating of snow or ice. Windmill blades will break off like matchsticks if they survive the violent storms that have grown as a result of Global Cooling.

So that the portion of mankind that survives the Covid-19 vaccine epidemic in the coming years can pee its pants. It will be very cold, but thanks to our government, we will no longer be able to consistently and affordably heat our houses with gas. Nuclear energy has also been banned. We will soon require extraordinary amounts of power and heat, yet these will be scarce (and what is available will be extremely expensive).

A human drama of unprecedented proportions is thus unfolding – a drama that could have been avoided if politicians had listened to real, independent science rather than bowing to a multimillionaire-controlled misanthropic UN/WEF/EU climate-vaccine elite and their environmental clubs and climate NGOs.

Chapter 4: The ticking time-bomb

Shutting off 'fossil' energy will cause unprecedented drama during new Little Ice Age

In spite of all the false CO2 / Global Warming propaganda, the scientific facts show time and time again that the dawn of the solar minimum has ushered in a period of Global Cooling, which will last at least several years, but probably several decades. What is less well known is that there is a ticking time bomb around the North Pole, which could go off literally at any time, and which could cause a very abrupt, catastrophic cooling of Europe. In the worst case scenario, a new Ice Age will even begin.

This ticking time bomb is the Beaufort Gyre, a huge wind-driven circling current in the Arctic Ocean, also known as the Arctic Ocean. This clockwise circulating water current exhibited a cyclical pattern in the second half of the 20th century, in which the current reversed itself every 5 to 7 years, temporarily turning counterclockwise. During this process, large amounts of ice and freshwater were pumped into the eastern Arctic Ocean and the northern Atlantic Ocean.

Severe winters 20th century and the Great Salinity Anomaly

During the 1960s and 1970s, this caused the upper layer (nearly a kilometer thick) of parts of the northern

Atlantic Ocean to cool. This is known as the Great Salinity Anomaly, which significantly disrupted the food chain in that part of the ocean. Many of Europe's extremely cold winters since 1951 occurred during this Great Salinity Anomaly.

There is increasing scientific evidence that not so much volcanoes, but this anomaly is the main trigger of ice ages. It happened once before in the 14th century. Climate scientists in the 1960s and 1970s predicted a new Ice Age for a reason. This was also taught in schools, even though the temperature drop since 1945 was the main argument for it.

What is going on now? The Beaufort Gyre has been rotating clockwise at a higher rate for more than 17 years. There has been no temporary reversal during that time. As a result, more and more fresh water has been attracted from melting sea ice, river water from Russia and North America, and the relatively fresh water from the Bering Sea.

'Ticking time bomb' may suddenly trigger new Ice Age

Scientists say the flow is going to reverse itself irrevocably, and at that point a huge amount of ice-cold water will spill into the Atlantic Ocean. Polar oceanographer Andrey Proshutinsky of the Woods Hole Oceanographic Institution called this a "ticking climate time bomb" back in 2014. Even if only 5% of that still increasing amount of ice water is released, the climate in Iceland and northern Europe could already cool temporarily.

If more than 5% is released, then the crucial Gulf Stream, the pillar of our temperate climate, could shut down. That will have catastrophic consequences for northern and western Europe, and plunge us abruptly, almost overnight, into a new (Little) Ice Age. 'The results strongly suggest that these things can happen suddenly thanks to the internal variability in the climate system,' warned Dr Martin Miles, researcher at the Institute of Arctic and Alpine Research at the University of Colorado. (1)

Closing off 'fossil' will cause unprecedented drama

The only thing that can then keep the population warm are gas, coal, oil and nuclear power plants. All of these, however, will be shut down. Windmills will break down or freeze due to extreme ice accretion, and/or bombard their accumulated ice accretion as concrete blocks on the surroundings within a radius of hundreds of meters or kilometers; solar panels will be continuously covered with ice, snow and/or frost. A tragedy of unprecedented proportions, with untold numbers of victims, thus seems to be in the making.

Chapter 5: Green deal damage

Is the rising number of wind farms to blame for the worsening drought? - According to a recent study, windmills are far more detrimental to public health than previously considered. - Renewable energy is a threat to the environment: 10 times the amount of minerals mined and 100 times the amount of land required than for fossil and nuclear energy

A comprehensive investigation done by a team of Irish and American-based academics, including members of CERES, the Center for Environmental Research and Earth Sciences, has been published in the scholarly journal Energies. The study comes to some startling findings concerning "green" energy policy, notably in the West. Wind farms and solar panel meadows, which the administration claims would dramatically transform the countryside, have a considerably greater negative impact on the ecology, climate, biodiversity, and human health than previously imagined. Despite this, trillions of euros and dollars are invested in them, with the populace receiving incredibly expensive and unstable electricity, as well as a damaged landscape and huge health concerns.

Between 2011 and 2018, the globe invested $3.66 trillion on climate change initiatives, with wind and solar power accounting for 55% and adaptations to extreme weather events accounting for the remaining 5%. Wind turbines and solar panels, the researchers discovered, can actually contribute to the problem they are designed to cure. Windmills raise the temperature at the bottom, causing bacteria to produce more CO2. And this is despite the fact that windmills are intended to replace CO2-emitting energy sources such as oil and gas.

(However, CO2 is not the issue; a greater temperature above ground causes more evaporation, and so dryness, when combined with the shifting air currents induced by windmills. And this is exactly what we've seen worsening in recent years in Europe, where windmills are being constructed at an alarming rate).

10 times more resources and 100 times more land are required.

'Sustainable' or 'green' energy takes up to ten times the amount of minerals as fossil energy. This mineral extraction is frequently accompanied by significant environmental damage. To replace merely 50 million of the 1.3 billion gasoline and diesel-powered automobiles with electric vehicles, worldwide cobalt, neodymium, and lithium output must be doubled, and more than half of all copper output must be used.

(The fundamental objective of climate globalists is thus not to replace all those automobiles, but to make auto travel so expensive that, as in the communist Eastern bloc, driving a car is only viable for a select privileged club. There aren't nearly enough raw materials available to supply batteries for that many automobiles, much alone recharge them using solely wind turbines and solar panels).

Solar panels and wind farms require 100 times the amount of land as fossil fuel power plants (which is why our farmers are being pushed or de facto expropriated under the premise of fabricated CO2 and nitrogen concerns). The government need their property for'renewable' energy production and housing construction). 'The ramifications of this land-use shift might be detrimental to biodiversity,' cautions the research team. 'Biomass consequences on biodiversity are substantially severe. The rising usage of biofuel crops like palm oil is already contributing to the loss of rainforests and other natural places (lett. 'habitats').

How much will it set you back? Only 3% of $2 trillion was deemed'sustainable.'

Wind and solar energy cost $2,000 billion globally between 2011 and 2018. Despite this, it only accounts for 3% of world energy consumption, compared to 85% for oil, gas, and coal. This begs the issue of how much it will cost to switch to 100 percent renewable energy. "And how long will that take?" Coiln hAiseadha, the chief researcher, wonders.

(The fundamental plan is the same as with auto traffic.) The EU aims to be entirely "carbon neutral" with 100 percent renewable energy by 2050 or 2055, but it doesn't inform us that overall energy output will have to be greatly reduced, because covering our whole continent with hundreds of millions of windmills and solar panels is unfeasible. This indicates that the people will face severe energy shortage. This is the purpose of your'smart' energy meters: to allow you to be rationed relatively quickly with a single computer order (assuming you can still pay your energy bill at all).

Renewable energy sources are unable to offer consistent energy 24 hours a day, seven days a week.

Engineers have long recognized that large-scale wind farms and solar panel fields are afflicted by the "intermittency" problem. Unlike fossil and nuclear energy, which supply consistent and reliable electricity 24 hours a day,'renewable' energy is based on the occurrence of wind and sunshine.

As a result, according to Dr. Ronan Connoly, "ordinary homes expect their refrigerators and freezers to operate continuously, and they may turn on the lights at any moment." Wind and solar proponents must recognize that they are incapable of delivering the constant 'on demand' power to which our modern culture is accustomed on a national scale.'

California, which is fast closing down fossil facilities and moving to wind and solar, and which wants entirely e-cars on the road by 2035, has already seen enormous 'blackouts,' leaving millions without power for hours.

33

Massive battery installations will not fix the problem.

This problem cannot be readily remedied with big-scale battery installations since it necessitates a big number of massive batteries that will take up several acres of land. Tesla has constructed a massive plant in South Australia. It has a capacity of 100 MW / 129 MWh and a land area of 1 hectare. According to a recent research, if the Canadian province of Alberta (population 4 million) shifts totally from coal to renewable energy, with natural gas and batteries as backup, 100 of these massive battery installations would be required to provide power at all times.

Other studies have found that the hardest cost of carbon (energy) taxes falls mostly on poorer households and rural inhabitants in the United States, Europe, and China.

Although it is claimed that this 'transition' is required to combat climate change (which is impossible anyway because the climate is always changing, is cyclical rather than linear, as government, media, and climate movements would have you believe, and is also 98 percent caused by the sun), only 5% of climate spending has been used for adaptation to changing conditions. However, the availability of cheap and dependable fossil energy is critical for constructing a resilient infrastructure and systems capable of responding promptly to disasters.

Mineral mining comes at a heavy cost to the local community.

The rapid expansion of mineral extraction also imposes a significant strain on the health of the local people. The health of mothers and children is jeopardized by unregulated cobalt mining. The extraction of lithium necessitates massive volumes of water, which can lead to pollution and water scarcity.

Aiseadha: *'The confrontation between the Standing Rock Sioux tribe and the Dakota Access pipeline has received widespread attention, but what about the effects of cobalt mining on indigenous peoples in the Democratic Republic of the Congo?'* And what about the effects of lithium mining on the people of the Atacama Desert? Do you recall the phrase yelled at Standing Rock? *'Wiconi! Water is vital to life! Well, just as it relates to the Sioux who are concerned about oil spills in the river, it also relates to the Atacama Desert's concerns about lithium poisoning of groundwater.'*

The complete evaluation by the scientific team, published on September 16 in a special edition of Energies, is 39 pages lengthy and is based on no less than 255 research publications on climate and energy.

Wind turbines have major health consequences.

Wind turbine building should be halted immediately as a result of new study. The effects for local inhabitants are far worse than previously thought. (And the climate lobby remains deafeningly silent on the hundreds of thousands of birds and bats who perish each year in the whirling sails.)

Wind turbine vibrations emit low-frequency (inaudible) noise that penetrates deep into the human body, causing sleep difficulties, tinnitus, headaches, memory and concentration loss, and stress. People who have cardiac difficulties are more prone to have a stroke or a heart attack. This is not "coincidence," as the climate lobby says, but has been proved and validated in over 300 global studies.

For these reasons, Germany maintains a minimum distance of one kilometer between wind turbines and dwellings. If politicians have their way, hundreds of additional windmills will be installed in the densely populated parts of Europe, far closer to dwellings. Aside from a few natural areas, there are few sites in our nation where there are no structures within a 2 km radius.

Windmills, get rid of them!

There can be no debate about the sheer devastation of the countryside caused by thousands of windmills. Again, we see the same tenebrous hypocrisy that characterizes climate activists: if a residential tower or bridge for a road is planned someplace, they scream blue murder about horizon pollution. However, now that massive windmills up to 300 meters tall are set to be installed, there is no opposition.

Windmills are a huge waste of money that only banks and manufacturers profit from. Worse, energy will become far more costly and unreliable for the average person. Furthermore, they do not benefit the climate or the ecosystem in any way; on the contrary, there is mounting evidence of the tremendous harm they inflict.

So, windmills, you're out! We can place bets on nuclear power and the development of Thorium power plants. Until then, we have more than enough clean gas and biofuel plants to supply our people with reliable and affordable energy for decades to come, as well as hundreds of billable hours.

Chapter 6: A cold future?

The New Great Solar Minimum (also known as the Eddy Minimum) anticipated by independent scientists began on June 8, 2020, according to a new scientific research conducted by astronomer and astrophysicist Valentina Zharkova, professor of applied mathematics at the British University of Northumbria.

According to Zharkova, all statistics point to a period of global cooling lasting until 2053, following which the sun will induce another protracted period of warming. The professor encourages governments to begin planning for poor crops and the need to heat their populations more aggressively.

According to Zharkova, new data on our star's magnetic field and accompanying solar activity reveal that "the Sun has initiated a current Grand Solar Minimum (2020-2053)." 'This will result in a large fall in magnetic field and activity, exactly as it did during the Maunder Minimum,' says the author.

Solar cycle 24 has now come to an end. That was the weakest cycle in almost a century. Cycle 25 started in 2020. 'Sunspots on the sun are frequently missing during periods of low solar activity, such as the current Great Solar Minimum. We have now noticed this; in 2020, there were 115 days without spots (= 78%), indicating that the Sun is on course to beat the 2019 record of 282 days without spots (= 77%).'

Deep freeze

Temperatures decreased considerably between 1645 and 1710, especially in the northern hemisphere, as the Sun entered a quiet phase known as the Maunder Minimum. The average temperature in Europe was 1.0 - 1.5 degrees Celsius cooler. 'Europe and North America slipped into deep freeze: glaciers extended across valley farmlands, sea ice penetrated as far south as the Arctic Circle, and rivers like the Dunab and the Thames often froze throughout these years.

This 'Little Ice Age' began in the 14th century and continued until the 18th century. The subsequent warming was not just a natural occurrence, but it was also highly needed.

According to all current evidence, the current Great Solar Minimum will last until cycle 27, or until 2053. The average temperature on Earth will fall by 1 degree Celsius, leaving it only 0.4 degrees warmer than in 1710. The largest temperature decline is projected during cycles 25 and 26 (2031) and cycles 26 and 27 (2032). (2042).

'International efforts are required to warm and nourish humankind.'

'The fall in global temperature over the next 30 years may have significant effects for different sections of the earth in terms of plant growth, agriculture, food supply, and heating demands, both in the northern and southern hemispheres,' adds the professor. All evidence of 'global warming' will be eliminated, which would need multilateral cooperation to handle heating and food supply issues for the whole world population.

All of the historically verified global cooling phenomena have been evident to everyone in recent years: weather extremes, big temperature variations, and drought in one region and too much water in another, with crop failures in an increasing number of areas.

Europe purposefully divides population protection from global cooling.

What a wonderful prospect that Europe would demolish its stable and affordable energy supply via natural gas, which is required for heating, and replace it with the still unreliable, extremely energy-inefficient, and, most all, extremely expensive wind and solar energy (and soon we will have no wood left either because our forests have been burned in biomass power stations). It's also good that the European government has launched war on the sophisticated agricultural and cattle industries at the same time.

The most vulnerable groups - the poor, the elderly, the chronically ill, and young children - are at risk of literally dying of cold and hunger over the next 30 years, either because they will no longer be able to pay their energy

40

bills or because it will simply be impossible to adequately heat and feed us. In other words, old habits die hard, especially when viruses prefer colder temperatures, resulting in widespread sickness and outbreaks.

We will and must continue to be blamed (= pay).

Meanwhile, our national climate propaganda agency par excellence, the KNMI, which receives millions of euros in funding, joyfully continues to teach the same rubbish that the climate is warming owing to human CO2 emissions. Because a complete tax system has been built on this deception, numerous companies benefit from 'green' government investments, and the now nearly 30 year old open UN plan to make 'climate warming' the pillar of a future, now in an advanced state of establishment, 'Agenda-21' communist world dictatorship, we will never, ever be told the truth, even when our rivers freeze over again in about 5 years.

Whatever occurs, man must and will continue to be blamed, because only man can pay taxes, and the sun, the true and sole source of climate change, simply does not bring in money, and does not care about the phony reality mandated by the worldwide climate sect.

The cold is spreading practically everywhere.

Meanwhile, the cold is spreading practically everywhere. The rescue of a party of chilled hikers in the Scottish Highlands, when the wind chill had plummeted to -10 C. at just under 1300 meters - MIN 10 degrees in August! - was overlooked by the media.

The whole United Kingdom had the coldest July since 1988, and the previous bank holiday weekend was also one of the worst on record. Last year, 33 degrees were reported on the same weekend, providing more proof of the advent of the Great Solar Minimum and the severe temperature fluctuations that it brings.

In August, there is also considerable snowfall in both the Alps and the Pyrenees. A total of 20 millimeters fell in the western Alps, closing numerous cable cars and hiking/biking trails. The glaciers in the Swiss resorts of Saas Fee and Zermatt have been restocked, allowing the ski season to begin in September. The same may be said about the well-known ski regions of Hintertux (Austria) and Passo Stelvio (Italy) (Italy).

On the other side of the world, in South Africa, the same scenes are playing out: unprecedented cold and snowfall plague South Africa - farmers and meteorologists are talking about the coldest winter in decades -, where the cable car to Table Mountain near Cape Town opened a few days earlier due to the "surprisingly" mentioned snowfall.

Beware, climate alarmists: the South Pole has 90 percent of all the ice on the planet. For years, Antarctica appears to be unconcerned with your bogus warming theories and forecast melting – on the opposite. There has not been nearly as much sea ice since records began 40 years ago, with 233,000 square kilometers more than typical. The rise by the end of August was higher than in 1979, and in all but four years, it was higher than in the whole 1980s and 1990s.

Residents on New Zealand's South Island were taken aback when a blanket of snow fell even on the lower slopes. 'My gosh, I've never encountered anything like this in my entire life,' said Blenheim resident Pam Wood. 'This much snow has never fallen before.' Again, the classic 'global cooling' extremes: until a few days ago, other meteorological stations in New Zealand had registered just half the typical quantity of snow. However, this was owing to a lack of humidity rather than a lack of temperature (it was chilly enough).

The period of strong solar activity and steady weather is coming to an end.

For over 100 years, high solar activity has produced a rather steady environment, allowing us to create our modern civilisation. However, because climate is cyclical rather than linear, it is always changing. Solar activity has now plummeted to roughly the level of the Dalton Minimum between 1790 and 1830, as anticipated by astronomers, which implies we could and should have been prepared for years.

In reality, the reverse has occurred and, sadly, continues to occur at an alarming rate. We will pay a colossal price for this diametric climate and energy policies in the next decades, because the sun will only begin to supply much-needed warmth to the world after 2053.

Chapter 7: Green deal depression

The 'Green Deal' of Brussels guarantees the 'economic death' of our once free and affluent continent - European media and politicians remain mute on the increasing worldwide escape, OUT of the Euro.

In his new report, 'The Fate of Europe,' top American economist Martin Armstrong 'dives into the shocking reality behind the scenes of the euro, and why it has failed to become a major reserve currency...

The coming crisis, like the Great Depression, will begin in Europe and spread like a contagious disease, eventually engulfing the global economy.

'One of the EU's worst faults has been to purposefully undermine democracy by depriving people of the chance to vote on their own destiny.'

'At the World Economic Conference in Rome, Nigel Farage called the World Economic Conferences we've been organizing since 1985 "the alternative to Davos."

When the euro was introduced, the Commission attended our World Economic Conference in London in 1997. Then I went into detail about how the euro should be constructed. The specific suggestions were then released.'

'The EU is meant to deny us the ability to vote on our destiny.'

'The entire architecture of the EU rests on the purposeful denial of any ability for people to decide on their own destiny.' Politicians have presumed that the public is TOO DUMB to know what is best for them.'

'For example, Germany, the backbone of the European economy, was NEVER given the chance to vote on the establishment of the euro. Chancellor (Helmut) Kohl subsequently conceded that he had acted like a tyrant, since if the German people had been allowed to vote on it, he would have lost by 7 votes to 3.'

'The EU appears to be committing economic death.'

'This study is critical for comprehending Europe's dangers.' The majority of people have no idea... because no European analyst working at one of the major financial institutions is ever permitted to criticize the EU or talk badly about the euro.' (1) As a result, you will hear practically nothing about the continuous foreign flight from the euro (to the dollar) caused by the ECB's years of negative interest rates (and more and more ordinary banks).

For the same reason, you won't hear much about Europe's stagnation, which is being caused by the decreasing economies of France and Italy (Q4 2019), as well as the drastically decreasing German car sector (last year -16 percent) to a 23-year low. 'Add to that the climate mania that has swept over Europe (the 'Green Deal, or the Climate Agreement), and they obviously appear to be on the approach of economic death in Europe,' says Armstrong.

'While politicians appear to be exclusively interested in transforming Europe into a new federal state, the underlying notion of the European Project demonstrates how dreadfully wrong they are.'

This means that the EU will either disintegrate or impose new charges on other member nations.

The historically reliable Economic Confidence Model (ECM) predicts a critical turning point for the euro(zone) in the fall of 2021. 'As we approach 2021, the pressure to keep the eurozone together will grow. Indeed, 2021/2022 appears to be a watershed moment for the global currency.'

According to the ECM, the final collapse of the whole West will come in 2032. Europe will have most likely crumbled by then.

'Civilization always fails because the left attempts to stifle the right.'

'The EU is the world's undisputed champion of regulation.'

In Western culture, the rule of law has crumbled. God is said to have written the Ten Commandments, which we have expanded into a billion laws. The more regulations there are, the more unfairness there is. A society dies because it becomes solely a conflict between two ideologies: the left constantly seeks to control the right, which merely wants to be free. This is why, in the end, all governments are buried in a same historical tomb.

Because society never learns from its errors, history keeps repeating itself.

'Perhaps that is why history must continue to repeat itself. We can only learn from our mistakes on an individual, intimate basis. Society as a whole appears incapable of learning such information. So we all poke our fingers in the candle flame over and over again, hoping for a different result each time. And, with each financial catastrophe, no one ever wonders if it has happened before, and if so, what the answer was. Those who do see the tendency are forced to watch others make the same mistakes over and over.

Chapter 8: Fossil fuel boycotts

Armstrong, the leading economist: 'Climate activists harm the economies' - Donald Trump: 'The alarmists always require the same thing: full authority in every part of our life to dominate, modify and control – let's be hopeful!'

The climate-hate girl Greta Thunberg shamelessly insulted by the liberal left-wing elite at the Globe Economy Forum in Davos said that our world was 'still on fire,' and so requires not a reduction in CO_2 emissions but an end to the development of all fossil fuels. Granting even half of her foolish wish would represent a complete breakdown of our modern society, claiming hundreds of millions of victims and sinking billions of people into deep poverty and wretchedness, partly because the climate is getting colder this year because the new minimum of solar power started.

"Climate activists are going to wreck the economy"

Martin Armstrong, America's top economist, sees it dreadfully. He has touch with folks in Davos who provide him background information. *'We can't do anything to prevent what's about to happen, I stated several times. World leaders will only act when the economy collapses and falls. Climate warriors will see to it that the economy is destroyed. They are socialists who want to penalize individuals for having their houses dry and heated."*

He says sarcastically with the photographs of the big blizzard in Newfoundland, *'This looks like global warming. Snowstorm a bit... Stay warm, Greta. Keep warm. You should actually turn off the heat. Don't worry about that! Don't worry about that! Right now, I can't suggest... 2020 marks the beginning of a new solar cycle, maybe a repetition of Little Ice Age, which might be weakest in at least 200 years. It's barely 10 degrees even here in Florida. I had to migrate further south for global warming."*

'Lower living standard' because of 'business opposed extremists'

'The misinformation about climate change has become a major economic issue weakening the world economy and decreasing the common person's level of living. It has been adopted solely by governments since it is the best technique of raising taxation.'

'Real extremists who are against the Industrial Revolution have drawn together this complete agenda. Jennifer Morgan (Greenpeace, the marionettes master of Greta) and Al Gore have been pulling through a very twisted theory with facts that are unsubstantiated, such as the claim that there is a 97% consensus (which is quite the contrary) and that cyclical oscillation from the late 19th century onwards has solely been caused by people, while refusing to look at the h

'The Eurozone'

'Their efforts to impose additional taxes and regulation on their notions, the EU's crazily costly 'Green Deal,' has caused Germany's economy to collapse and has swept away the whole Eurozone. When they were to be carefully researched, Gore and Morgan colluded to silence any detractors of their motion. It now seems like a quest for a witch."

'A really profound turning point will be 2020, even retrospectively.' The lowest solar cycle is expected to reach its peak in 2025 by NASA in 200 years. 'And if the volcanic explosion (one of the symptoms of global cooling) rises sharply, two or three more outbreaks might lead to a volcanical winter which would boost food prices substantially.'

Can economic and social suicide in Europe continue to be stopped?

Future generations will long consider how leaders of the once great civilisation in Europe could lose their common sense by putting into law the ravings of a mentally disturbed girl and committing economic and social suicide through the destruction, death and destruction of their own historically unprecedented, prosperous industrial societies.

51

Unless we alter direction significantly via the voting stand by 2021 at the latest. Can that still be? Martin Armstrong has already given up hope and thinks – like more and more experts - that first we will have to face a protracted and catastrophic catastrophe, and clean our society from the prevalent green ideal of the Marxist climate.

Donald Trump: The prophets of doom must be rejected and remain hopeful

In Davos, though, one international leader sounds a healthy dissent: US President Donald Trump. "It is not a pessimistic period, but an optimist moment... We need to reject these endless doom prophets and their predictions of a (climate) catastrophe in order to embrace tomorrow's possibility. They would like us to do badly, but we will not. In the sixties, overpopulation, mass death and the end of oil were anticipated in the seventies. They forecasted overpopulation.

'These alarmists constantly require that we have the entire authority to govern all aspects of our life and modify them. But we will never allow extreme socialists to damage, spoil or erase our country's freedom. America is always the great, powerful and unwavering stronghold of liberty."

Top economist Armstrong: 'Nature proves climate alarmists are outright liars' - Freakish weather not caused by CO2, but onset of solar minimum and global cooling, and a shift in the magnetic north pole

The mainstream media now assigns all erratic weather phenomena, such as the wildfires in Australia, to climate change. With misleading, manipulated short-term statistics, the naive Western population is kept under the delusion that the climate is warming extremely fast, while just the opposite is true. 'Climate change has become a fanatical religion,' writes top American economist Armstrong. There is no evidence, it is based entirely on faith.... It is Europe that seems destined to collapse by all the climate measures'.

The EU's 'Green Deal' is going to cost taxpayers at least €1.2 trillion until 2030, but all sorts of 'additional investments' in the order of hundreds of billions of euros will be added to that. Once again, all kinds of different amounts and years are deliberately thrown around to keep Europeans confused about the real, monstrous amounts that Brussels is going to spend on the rapid destruction of a large part of our prosperity and almost all of our freedoms, because energy and (private) transport will soon become unaffordable.

More than 410,000 jobs are at risk in the German auto industry, and this is just the beginning of the deliberate de-industrialization of Europe spearheaded by the Marxist European Commission. *'Among the people I speak to in the German car industry, the general consensus is that they will be driven into bankruptcy before there is any recognition that it's all nonsense,'* Armstrong said.

Solar minimum causes volcanic activity, major danger to crops

Increasing volcanic activity (e.g. Mexico, Philippines) is one piece of evidence that we have entered a solar minimum. Five or six medium-sized eruptions, or one large one, could seriously accelerate the cooling, pushing us into "a volcanic winter. Harvests will then fail en masse, and millions of people will die of starvation and all kinds of epidemics.

Historical examples abound. For example, in the 6th century, half the population in Scandinavia died out due to a series of volcanic eruptions in America and Iceland (between 536-547 AD). The entire northern hemisphere was darkened, causing abrupt climate change and very rapid cooling. Historian Procopius wrote that in the Byzantine Empire, even for a full year, the sun gave off only a faint glow, no stronger than the moon under normal conditions.

In China, it snowed in the summer, and all crops failed between 536-539 AD. In Europe, the volcanic winter marked the beginning of the "Dark Ages" with nearly a century of chronic famine. In the Eastern Roman Empire, bubonic plague broke out, killing one-third to one-half of all people.

'Nature proves it's outright liars'

It is very easy for the 'global warming' church to claim that, for example, the Australian forest fires were caused by CO2 climate change. 'They only make a connection with CO2, but there is ZERO (scientific and historical) evidence for that. If it were really caused by humans, then the historical data should show that this kind of thing did not occur before the industrial revolution. But they ignore the historical fact that the climate has always changed. They don't even want to respond to that, and the mainstream media just take their claims as indisputable facts, without doing even a little research.'

For example, Australia experienced several even worse fires and droughts in the 19th century and early 20th century. 'But these activists (and politicians) claim that everything is due to CO2, without any proof, and people accept everything they say... Nature itself shows that these people are outright liars.'

Climate activists 'are like the barbarians who brought down the Roman Empire'

'I am concerned that we are entering a solar minimum that will be the deepest since the Little Ice Age some

200+ years ago. The climate change fanatics have elevated their claims to the level of a religious belief... These climate activists (plus the European establishment politics) will not listen to reason. Anyone who dares to contradict them is immediately attacked and demonized by them. With the help of a 16 year old girl, of whom they dare to claim she is a climate authority, they managed to infiltrate governments and DAVOS (World Economic Forum).'

'The climate activists, with their extreme behavior, seem to have adopted the role of the enemy from the time when the pagans overthrew the Roman Empire. Indeed, they also claimed that society was doomed because the Christians refused to worship their (nature's) gods... The climate became colder, resulting in southward mass migration. The Romans called them the barbarians.'

'We are now seeing the same kind of division, with intense hatred of anyone who tries to contradict the climate activists. (Traditional) religions are declining, while progressivism (Marxism) is getting stronger. The core of climate activists want to destroy modern society because they blame the industrial revolution for the warming after 1850, which was a normal cycle because we just came out of the Little Ice Age.'

In the West, especially in Europe, we are now seeing 'a very similar collision that divided the Roman Empire, and set in motion its eventual fall. We are again entering a solar minimum, with the risk of cold weather resulting in huge mass starvation deaths.'

Unprecedentedly fast shift in magnetic North Pole

That process could be reinforced by the unprecedentedly rapid shift of the magnetic North Pole. From a few kilometers per year, this shift towards Siberia has accelerated in a very short time to about 50 to 60 kilometers per year.

The remains of suddenly frozen mammoths and other prehistoric animals have previously shown that about 42,000 years ago they fell victim to a lightning-fast, catastrophic cooling that probably took only a few days or hours, and was probably the result of such a pole shift. It is certainly not said that this will happen again now, but the unexpected acceleration of the displacement of the magnetic North Pole has taken the entire science by surprise.

It may be, therefore, that even before 2030 it will turn out that Europe's diametrically disastrous climate policy will have contributed enormously to the widespread misery that will result from global cooling-related crop failures, epidemics, and the by then largely dismantled reliable and affordable energy supply with fossil fuels and nuclear power plants.

Chapter 10: The worst deal ever

The European Commission's Green New Deal and the Climate Czar Frans Timmerman are sounding an alert from a German farmer. By 2050, Brussels wants to see Europe become so called 'climate neutral,' and this requires the elimination of industrial agriculture. If this proposal passes, inefficient, considerably less "green" agriculture, lower crops and thus higher food costs would result. Hunger and poverty, particularly among lower income individuals, will become commonplace.

More information was disclosed in May on the 'European Green Deal.' The European Commission wishes to reverse society entirely and to make the transition fair and inclusive for all. But at least one group is totally excluded: farmers.

'Farm to Fork' is the moniker for Europe's agricultural reform initiative. German farmer Marcus Holtkötter for the Global Farmer Network believes that the objectives of this plan are entirely "unrealistic." 'Farmers should halve their crop protection products and fertilizers should decrease by 20 percent over the next decade. Used as 'organic' crop, up to a fourth of the current cropland.

"Anyone of this would, of course, upset the foods of people," added the farmer sarcastically.

'Food is going to be cheaper'

Europeans are fortunate with enough of nourishment (although quality might be questioned, particularly for processed food), particularly as agriculture may be considered one of the world's most modern and effective. The ground is fertile and the harvest is nearly always high. 'We have obtained outstanding results because of intensive farming. As a consequence we have no hunger and malnutrition problems, which in other civilizations torment individuals with less fortunate.'

'There are lower harvests presently being proposed by the European Commission. This leads to one thing for customers directly: greater pricing. It's going to make food more costly.'

More and more tiny crops

Another major concern is that farmers already in difficulty would get even less from reduced yields and thus decreased sales. 'The Committee does not comprehend that a poor approach to agriculture will force farmers to quit. The lesser yields are much less once this happens."

That is the antithesis of what is said by the Committee, which is 'sustainable' agriculture and economy. More importantly, if Europe's farmers are no longer able to produce enough, there is the question of where our food should come from then. Consequently, in nations with fewer fertile and productive land the European Green Deal will unavoidably lead to even more wasteful agriculture.

'What is 'green' for less crops to grow on greater soil?'

'This may fill Europe's belly with fewer farmers and perhaps even assuage Brussels's consciences of campaigners and bureaucrats. But it won't assist the climate at all. Our objective should be to increase food supplies on less land. In fact, the EU method, led not by research but by dogma, will lead to fewer foods growing on more land. What about the "green?"

Note that the population of the planet would have expanded by 2 billion more by 2050. by 2050. You've got to eat too. That would be a job, but it could still happen, with the present effective farming practices. In recent decades, agriculture has proved highly inventive.

The EU sees us as a problem

But more laws and more limitations are NOT what farmers need. This would be the ultimate blow to many and jeopardize food security in Europe. What appears worst is that the European Green Deal assumes that agriculture is the enemy of conservation in nature. It considers us instead of an ally in a shared cause as a problem to be resolved."

'We are working hard to be as green as we can. On my property, with solar panels, we create some of our power. In the fertilization and weed control, we employ GPS and other technology. To safeguard the soil, we grow crops against erosion. We are planting floral beds to attract crop pollinating insects and boost biodiversity.'

"It's best to ensure that farmers cannot reach goals to avoid beneficial innovation. The European Green Bargain is a terribly awful deal for farmers and all the others.

With some flowers and plants growing in fields or in forests (if they are not biomass-cutting), now more important than ensuring that all the citizens can put sufficient and affordable food on the table, only a popularly-provoked revolution can still prevent hundreds of thousands of European farmers from begging.

Chapter 11: Great green reset

'Bribed politicians push their Green Agenda on people undemocratically - this is the worst policy plan in history!' - 'The New Normal, the actual one? You must stay at home with a minimum basic income and solely watch TV'

The economic harm inflicted by the bogus corona-security, an influenza-like virus yet bogus, is enormous. In Germany, 21% of enterprises (even 85% of tourists) said they fear they won't be able to survive in the next few months. This devastation, purposefully launched by the elite, of the "old economy, is part of the planned Grand Green Reset that would create the Marxist New World Order. The immunization of the whole world's population, which aims to stop and even reverse population increase, constitutes an essential aspect of this Plan.

Fossil fuel economy will be destroyed for Zero-CO2

According to Armstrong, "A rich and well-organized worldwide coalition is not only trying, since it does not vaccinate China and Russia, to force vaccination and depopulate the globe, which is tactical, but also destroys the world economy to eliminate fossil fuels. They push through the notion of how the world might work to avert climate change by bribery and conspiracy, and via a mandate that imposes zero CO2.'

"We shall see mass unemployment as they remove industries and keep people at risk to minimize CO2. Britain required less electricity for two months, and the coal facilities were shut down. There is an unsold flood of automobiles. The heart failed. The heart failed. South Europe will not survive without large rescue projects. They have paralyzed tourism. This is going to make the whole debt issue crazy."

Gates creates a planetary population reduction vaccine.

'With two types of vaccinations, the first is a normal vaccination, in which a bit of the virus is injected. But Gates also finances vaccinations that act very differently and modify your genetic DNA to protect you from Covid-19.

'Many politicians, like Kohl, can be bribed' ' '

'The majority of the people do not know that former German Chancellor Helmut Kohl stated that when he introduced the euro, he acted like a tyrant, denying it the right of German people to vote. In 2000, he took enormous shrimps and was alienated from him by his CDU party. After his death, Swiss Bank accounts and cash transactions on parking lots were uncovered with concealed million.

'The euro has thus been established out of the democratic process by this complete corruption. The same method is again being utilized to ensure that politicians take up this (Green) agenda which is targeted at the ordinary people. Many will establish that they were bribed afterward."

'Soft Soviet Revolution'

Armstrong now calls a Soft Soviet Revolution. What is going on? These folks believe that they can easily influence the international economy. Their major purpose is to remove Trump, who they consider to be the biggest obstacle to thwart this worldwide coup."

'It's a big operation to get rid of Trump to get the US on its global agenda. He will never vote against his own interests because he owns private corporations. However, career politicians have nothing but the state's unending permits. This is a big distinction and why professional politicians never protect the public. That's the reason. It remains to be seen if after 2024 elections will take place. They are trying to put an end to democracy.

"The New Socialist Green World Order: the most evil plan ever?"

'Governments are aware that in terms of debt, they are at no return point. As early as 2014, the ECB has adopted negative rates. After six years of disastrous Keynesian programs, they now understand the collapse of the global debt system and socialism. They hope that they will utilize the virus to kill all 'fossil' jobs and recompense people for their minimum basic universal income. This is the true "New Standard"!

"It is in every respect that this report (the Great Reset) takes into consideration and documents their agenda, for example by wishing to increase taxes by 400 per cent, and by introducing the guaranteed (universal) basic earnings (UBI) for all those people they leave work to stay home just to watch TV."

Armstrong ends, "Welcome to the New Green Socialist World Order." 'The 'Great Reset' is portrayed strategically. It is arguably the most ridiculous political plan ever devised to deny all people of human rights intentionally, so that we can only exist (to continue to be) by grace. There may not have been such a more evil conspiracy throughout human history.'

Our other books

Check out our other books for other unreported news, exposed facts and debunked truths, and more.

Join the exclusive Rebel Press Media Circle!

You will get new updates about the unreported reality delivered in your inbox every Friday.

Sign up here today:

https://campsite.bio/rebelpressmedia